More GREAT WESTERN STEAM in South Wales

MORE GREAT WESTERN STEAM IN SOUTH WALES

S. RICKARD

D. BRADFORD BARTON LIMITED

Frontispiece

Photographed through the archway of a bridge that carries the single line St. Fagans to Tyn-y-caeau Junction connection, 2-8-2 tank No. 7232 coasts along the main line towards St. Fagans with an eastbound freight.

printed in Great Britain by Chapel River Press (IPC Printers), Andover, Hants. for the publishers

D. BRADFORD BARTON LTD · Trethellan House · Truro · Cornwall · England

introduction

This volume is a sequel to *Great Western Steam in South Wales* and compiling it has been a somewhat more arduous task than was the case with its predecessor. To have produced something of a very similar nature would have been easy but it was intended that the contents of *More Great Western Steam in South Wales* should be regarded as supplementary or complementary to its forerunner, rather than simply another version.

For the sake of variety the progression has been reversed this time, working from Swansea towards Severn Tunnel Junction and more emphasis has been given to the Newport and Severn Tunnel districts. There are many new locations, and where the locations are similar the angles have been varied. Classes of locomotives presented are of necessity similar, although this volume includes one of the last of the 'Saints', together with one of the little-known Taff Vale 'H' class.

With the exception of the Brecon & Merthyr Railway, lines of the major pre-grouping companies still carry passenger traffic. Of the minor companies, the only survivor in this category is the Cardiff Railway. Time has moved on and today we have reached the stage where names like Rhondda & Swansea Bay Railway and South Wales Mineral Railway can scarcely be recalled by the travelling public. Younger readers of the volume will have probably never seen a locomotive of the pre-grouping companies on routine work, as the last of them disappeared in 1957.

To those who saw and travelled behind these locomotives, this volume will provide pleasant memories and to those that have not it may well kindle their interest in a time when motive power was more varied than in these standardised days.

'Hall' class 4-6-0
No. 6985 *Parwick Hall*
blasts up the bank
through the industrial
area between Swansea
(High St.) and Landore
with a Sunday
Swansea–Paddington
express in 1958.

At the same location,
easier progress is
made by No. 7912
Little Linford Hall as it
makes for Landore
shed in the company
of a 'Britannia' class
Pacific after they had
worked expresses into
Swansea.

A Stephenson Locomotive Society Special at Tonmawr Junction in charge of 5700 class 0-6-0 pannier tank No.5734 on 29 May 1954, Tonmawr Junction was on the former South Wales Mineral Railway.

The same Special at Maesteg (Neath Road). This location is on the truncated remains of the former Port Talbot Railway, which latterly served the pits at Cwmdu.

4200 class 2-8-0 tank No. 4246 passes Pyle West Junction on the main line with a west-bound freight in the winter of 1956. This was the western junction for the Porthcawl branch.

One of the 'County' class 4-6-0s introduced into South Wales after the war, No. 1020 *County of Monmouth* passes Pyle West Junction with a Fishguard Harbour to Paddington parcels train, January 1956.

Pyle West Junction again, as an engineers' inspection train arrives in charge of 1933-designed 5700 class 0-6-0 pannier tank No. 9664.

At Porthcawl station sidings, return excursion trains wait in the summer of 1960, shortly after a thunderstorm. Porthcawl is a popular holiday resort in South Wales to which such trains were run from most places in the Valleys as well as from further afield. The branch lost its passenger service in 1964.

A main line connection for Porthcawl leaves Pyle in June 1955, propelled by auto-fitted 2-6-2T No. 5555. Locomotives of this 4500 class were specially fitted for auto working in South Wales with the introduction of regular interval passenger services in 1953.

A Swansea–Manchester express enters Bridgend, on the main line, headed by 'Castle' class No. 7021, *Haverfordwest Castle* on a summer Saturday in 1962.

There was also a fairly intensive freight service on the Porthcawl Branch, most of which came from the limestone quarries at Cornelly, and was bound for Margam Steel Works; Duty U14 of Tondu shed, consisting of 5700 class pannier tank No. 7762 and brake van, at the quarries on a Saturday afternoon in 1962.

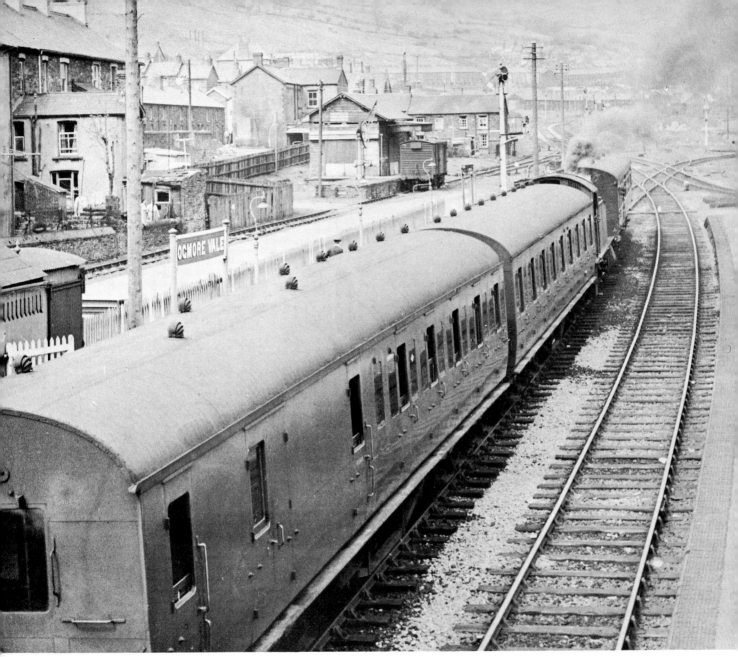

Ogmore Vale Station, on the branch to Blaengwynfl; 4500 class 2-6-2 tank No. 5524 waits with an afternoon train from Bridgend on 3 May 1958.

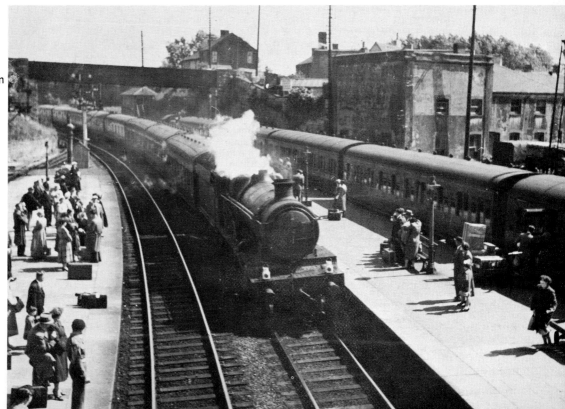

Two views on the main line at Bridgend. 5700 class pannier tank No. 8740 in the bay platform on a Stephenson Locomotive Society Special Train in 1954 and (below) a busy scene as 'Grange' class No. 6818 *Hardwick Grange* arrives with a westbound express. A connecting train for the Vale of Glamorgan line waits in the bay, 3 July 1954.

On the Vale of Glamorgan line at Rhoose, 0-6-2 tank No.5664 shunts the sidings near the cement works.

5600 class 0-6-2 tank No.6663 leaves Barry Island with the empty stock of an Eastern Valleys excursion. Collins' fairground can be seen on the right; May 1954.

Biglis Junction on the former Barry Railway. Looking west as 5100 class 2-6-2 tank No. 4162 heads a passenger train for Cardiff. In the background is Cadoxton, junction for the former Barry Railway main line to the Rhondda Valley. Looking east (below) the same train returns later, heading for Barry Island. Biglis Junction had its own signal box until after World War II; thenceforward the junction was controlled from nearby Cadoxton box.

Sunday diversions at Dinas Powis. When engineering work was in progress on the main line, trains were diverted via the former Barry and Vale of Glamorgan lines. In the upper photograph 'Hall' class No. 5937 *Stanford Hall* heads west with a freight. Below, 'Castle' class No. 5082 *Swordfish* eases through with a South Wales–Paddington express, 30 January 1955.

Penarth Town station on the former Taff Vale Railway. Once a through route between Cardiff and Barry, this has now become a terminus for trains from Cardiff. A 6400 class pannier tank waits hopefully for traffic.

A general view of Barry Shed, once a haven for 0-6-0 and 0-6-2 tanks of various pre-grouping companies.

A 5600 class 0-6-2 tank takes a run at the 1 in 40 Penarth bank on the former Taff Vale Railway, with a train from Cardiff in the autumn of 1952.

'Grange' class No. 6828 *Trellech Grange* heads a westbound express through Llantrisant. Pannier tank No. 4674 waits in the bay with a Penygraig branch train.

Llantrisant was the junction for a branch line to Pontypridd, on which a freight train is seen at Cowbridge Road Crossing—the 11.00 a.m. Llantrisant to Pontypridd coke ovens, headed by 5600 class 0-6-2T No. 5618 and banked by pannier tank No. 3617; 13 May 1958.

2800 class 2-8-0 No. 2866 working hard through rural scenery between St. Fagans and Ely as it moves an eastbound freight.

On the main line, the down South Wales Pullman approaches Peterston on a rainy day in November 1955, headed by 'Castle' class 4-6-0 No. 7001 *Sir James Milne*.

26

4200 class 2-8-0T No.5254 approaches St. Georges crossing on the main line with a down freight. Below, near Ely (Main Line) an unidentified 'Castle' makes a spirited departure from Cardiff with a Paddington–South Wales express.

Illuminated by the late evening sun, the 6.50 p.m. Porthcawl–Newport stopping train
leaves St. Fagans headed by one of the 8400 class pannier tanks.

'Castle' class 4-6-0 No. 5060 *Earl of Berkeley* heads a Paddington–South Wales train near St. Fagans, 30
September 1957.

A Hall class 4-6-0 crossing the River Ely near St. Fagans with an up stopping train.

Although leaking steam, No. 7012 *Barry Castle* makes a strong exit from St. Fagans, as it heads a Carmarthen–Cheltenham stopping train.

A down iron ore train for Margam steel works approaches Ely (Main Line) in charge of a 4200 class 2-8-0 tank.

Another bridge across the River Ely, this time nearer Ely (Main Line), as a 'Hall' makes its way across with an up stopping train; No. 5955 *Garth Hall* was a regular on this section.

There are two Waterhall junctions in South Wales, neither of them very well known. This one is on the former Taff Vale Railway on the western outskirts of Cardiff. Auto-fitted 4500 class 2-6-2T No. 4572, sandwiched between three coaches, is heading for Radyr Sidings after bringing in a football excursion to Ninian Park Platform, Cardiff, in 1956.

Not far away from Ninian Park Platform are Canton Sidings from which a Swansea–Old Oak Common empty van train leaves in charge of 2800 class No. 2805 in August 1956.

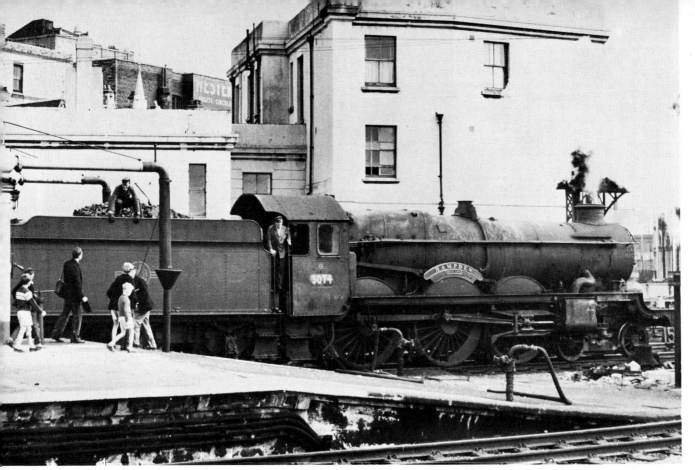

A 'Castle' class which had seen better days, No.5074 *Hampden*, about to leave Cardiff (General) with an excursion for Clifton Zoo in 1964. She had been withdrawn from service and later reinstated. At this time shedded at Cardiff (East Dock), her number and name plates had been removed to prevent theft by souvenir hunters and others. At this time, obviously, the number plates could not be found.

One of the last of the 'Saints', 2920 *St. David* at Cardiff (General) in February 1953, shortly before withdrawal, at the head of a Hereford train.

The down 'Pembroke Coast Express' waits at Cardiff (General) on a dull January day in 1958. 'Castle' class No.5077 *Fairey Battle* is at the head.

Cardiff (Queen Street) station, the gateway to the valleys, on the former Taff Vale Railway. Above, looking south as 5600 class 0-6-2 T No. 6626 enters with a Rhymney Valley passenger train, Queen Street South Signal Box in the background. Below, the north end of the station as another 5600 class enters with a down Rhymney line passenger train, 31 January 1959.

7200 class 2-8-2 tank No. 7203 lifts a freight up the l in 75 gradient into Cardiff (General).

4500 class 2-6-2 tank No.5572 moves out of Rhiwbina Halt with a Cardiff (Bute Road) to Coryton Halt train in August 1957. This line on the former Cardiff Railway served the residential areas on the northern outskirts of Cardiff.

5100 class 2-6-2 tank No. 4164 enters Heath Halt (High Level) with a Rhymney Valley train in March 1958.

Two views of pre-grouping locomotives approaching Heath Halt (High Level). No. 367 of the Taff Vale 'A' class heads an up passenger train on a summer's evening in July 1953 and (below) No. 83, a Great Western rebuild of a Rhymney Railway passenger tank, heads for Llanbradach Colliery on a winter day in the mid. 1950s.

Cherry Orchard Wagon Works are in the background as 5600 class No.5635 heads up the Rhymney Valley with a train of empties in 1963.

Heath Junction, looking towards Cardiff, as 5600 class No.6614 approaches with a train of empties, 8 April 1964. Below, looking towards Caerphilly, as the same train passes.

No.6682 of the 5600 class blasts its way out of Llanishen with a Cathays Shed lunch-time working from Cardiff to Caerphilly and back, January 1957.

A Cardiff (Canton) turn, 'H14,' works the long drag up to Caerphilly Tunnel in 1963, with a train of empties. 5600 class No.6689 is at the he

PASSENGERS MUST
NOT CROSS THE LINE
EXCEPT BY MEANS
OF THE BRIDGE

An interesting survivor of the Taff Vale Railway. 'H' class 0-6-0T No.193 was one of a class consisting of three locomotives only, specially built for working the Pwllyrhebog Incline in the Rhondda Valley. The photograph was taken at the tar distillery in Caerphilly during 1956 when the locomotive was owned by the NCB.

On a bright spring morning in 1956, 5600 class No.5605, in resplendent condition, leaves Cefn On Halt with a down Rhymney Valley passenger train.

5600 class No. 5653 emerges from under the bridge at the north end of Caerphilly station, with an up work-men's train in August 1954.

In 1956 the Gloucester Railway Society organised a South Wales Rail Tour. No. 391, ex-TV 'A' class is seen passing Caerphilly station on this, en route to Cardiff via the roundabout way of Walnut Tree Viaduct, after visiting Caerphilly Works.

5100 class 2-6-2 tank
No.4101 heads a down
Rhymney Valley train
near Hengoed on
23 February 1956. The
line in the extreme top
left is the Aberdare to
Pontypool route, on
which the next four
photographs were
taken.

The massive stone
structure of Hengoed
Viaduct with a 5600
class 0-6-2 T passing
over with an eastbound
freight.

5700 class 0-6-0 PT
No.3685 leaves
Pontllanfraith (Low
Level) with a west-
bound local, October
1956.

Maesycwmmer Junction looking west, with a pannier tank running round a short freight train. The lines diverging right lead down to the former Brecon & Merthyr line between Newport and Brecon.

Maesycwmmer Junction looking east; 5600 class 0-6-2 T No.6651 heads west-wards with a freight.

No. 35, an ex-Rhymney
Railway 0-6-2 tank
waits to enter Bargoed
Pits as a 5600 class
tank leaves.

No. 40, a Great
Western Railway
rebuild of the type of
Rhymney Railway
locomotive seen above,
enters the relief line
at Cherry Orchard
Sidings with a down
freight from Cwm
Bargoed in September
1952. Two other
locomotives of this
class, Nos. 39 and 44,
were rebuilt by the
Great Western.

No.36, of the former Rhymney Railway, shunts in characteristic scenery at Bargoed Pits on 9 May 1957.

Just above Bargoed Pits, pannier tank No. 9616 leaves Bargoed station with an afternoon passenger train for Dowlais on 2 May 1959.

On the Roath branch of the former Taff Vale Railway, No. 373, a former Taff Vale 'A' class heads a train of empties from Cardiff Docks to the Valleys.

Maindy Halt, in its heyday had only a peak period service to Cardiff (Bute Road) and even this was withdrawn soon after this photograph was taken in 1957; a Valleys train passes through with No. 5691 at the head.

An unusual sight at Heath Halt (Low Level) in 1952, as No. 35 of the former Rhymney Railway heads a train of empties for Nantgarw Colliery. Shortly afterwards a new connection to the colliery was opened off the Taff Vale Cardiff–Pontypridd line and workings via Heath Halt (Low Level) ceased.

Pentyrch Crossing on the former Taff Vale Cardiff–Pontypridd section on 8 February 1958. An Abercynon turn worked by 5600 class No. 5699 is heading up the Valleys with a train of empties.

Pentyrch Crossing from another angle, with the delightful Castell Coch on wooded hills in the background. Pannier tank No. 4678 heads a short freight towards Cardiff.

The frequently photographed Walnut Tree Viaduct dominates the scene as 5600 class 0-6-2T No. 5687 passes underneath with a working from Cardiff (Cathays) shed.

A pannier tank heads a down train from Nantgarw Colliery and leaves the Nantgarw branch by the line referred to on page 60.

0-6-2T No.5627 approaches Taffs Well on the down relief line with a freight train. For some ten miles between Pontypridd and Cardiff, the former Taff Vale Railway had four tracks, and in the early 1900s coal trains were nose to tail over the whole length of this section.

A distant view, in which the location of the preceding photograph can just be seen, as a former Rhymney Railway 0-6-2T enters the branch with a train for Nantgarw Colliery.

A train for Cardiff Docks leaves the Nantgarw branch, once part of the Cardiff Railway main line, headed by ex-Rhymney Railway 0-6-2 tank No.35 in November 1956.

Upper Boat power station provides the background as 5600 class tank No. 5643 passes with a down train on the former Taff Vale Pontypridd to Cardiff section, 25 October 1956.

North of Upper Boat is Maesmawr where 5100 class 2-6-2T No. 4163 heads for Barry Island with a holiday excursion train in the summer of 1960.

5600 class 0-6-2T No.5695 on the 1 in 69 bank to Tonteg Junction, in the summer of 1960, with an excursion from the valleys to Barry Island, via the former Barry Railway main line.

Dean 0-6-0 No. 2538 at the head of a Gloucestershire Railway Society special near Nantgarw Halt, between P.C. and N junction and Penrhos Junction in May 1956. Regular passenger services were withdrawn from this section shortly afterwards and now even freight trains no longer run, as the track has been lifted.

A general view of Pontypridd station. A 5600 class 0-6-2 tank is coming into the scene with a train of empties. Some of these will be shunted off at Maritime Colliery, the entrance to which can just be seen at the end of the platforms.

Another scene at Nantgarw shortly before withdrawal of passenger services in 1956. 6400 class 0-6-0 pannier tank No.6411 departs with an afternoon Pontypridd to Caerphilly auto-train.

Dinas in the Rhondda Valley. A Saturday afternoon freight eases through the station in charge of 8400 class 0-6-0 PT No.8419.

On the Aberdare to Pontypool Road line, 5100 class 2-6-2 tank No.5103 heads a Neath–Pontypool Road train towards Quakers Yard (High Level) Tunnel in October 1958.

5600 class 0-6-2 tank No.5615 vigorously attacks the 1 in 220 gradient out of Nelson and Llancaiach on to the branch for Dowlais (Cae Harris) with a freight from Aber Junction.

In August 1957 a down passenger train from Merthyr enters Abercynon station, junction for the Aberdare and Merthyr lines.

An engine and brake van leaving Pontcynon Junction on the former Taff Vale line to Aberdare (Low Level), September 1958.

A Churchward mogul coasts over Quakers Yard Viaduct with a westbound freight in March 1958. The second viaduct to the rear was on the Great Western and Rhymney Railway Joint Line to Merthyr, closed at this time due to its unsafe condition.

'Hall' class No. 5961 *Toynbee Hall* makes light work of a four coach train as it heads through Rumney for Bristol, January 1953.

A 'Hall' Class 4-6-0 caught broadside on as it hurries through Rumney with down passenger train.

A rather unusual main line sight at Rumney—a 1400 class 0-4-2 tank emerges from the morning mist with a Newport–Cardiff local in the winter of 1952.

The down 'Pembroke Coast Express' drifts along the level section near Rumney in charge of 'Castle' class No. 7009 *Athelney Castle* on 1 June 1954.

Framed by the signals of St. Mellons West box, 'Hall' class No.6999 *Capel Dewi Hall* approaches with an up local passenger in the autumn of 1952.

Ebbw Junction on the main line, looking towards Newport Tunnel; 'Hall' class No. 4979 *Wootton Hall* approaches with a down passenger train, 23 August 1954.

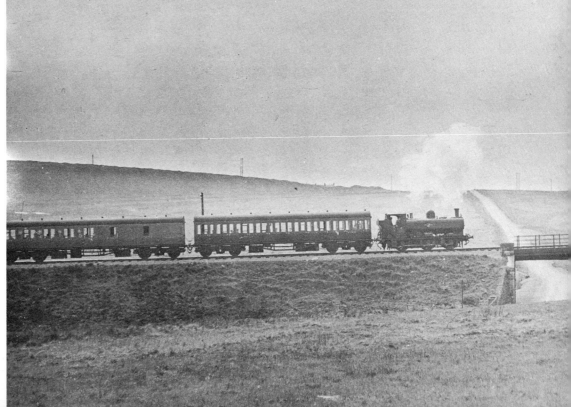

Two scenes on the former Brecon & Merthyr line. Above, a Brecon to Newport train approaches Pengam (Mon) with 5700 class 0-6-0 pannier tank No. 3691 in charge, 9 May 1959, whilst (below) a pannier tank works hard on the gradient out of Fochriw, making for Brecon through wild and desolate country, on the same day.

In the autumn of 1953 the Stephenson Locomotive Society ran a special train over the Eastern and Western Valley lines, consisting of 0-6-0 pannier tank No. 6403 and an auto-set. It is seen (left upper) at Newport Dock Street, (left lower) Panteg and Griffithstown, (above) Pantywaun and overleaf at Ebbw Vale (High Level). The latter two were in former London & North Western territory.

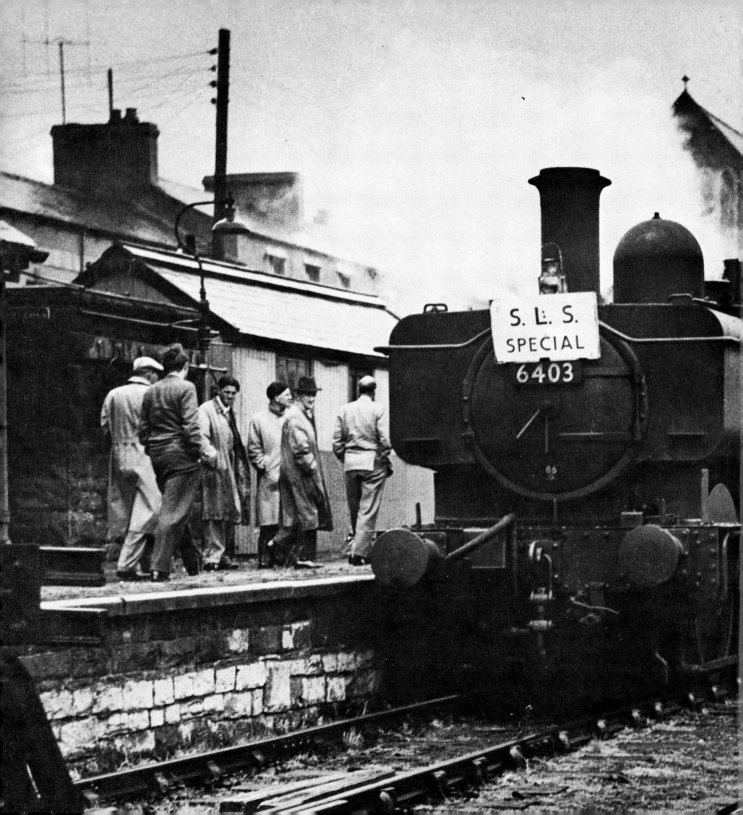

'Castle' class 4-6-0 No. 7012 *Barry Castle* emerges from Newport Tunnel and approaches Gaer Junction with the down 'Pembroke Coast Express' in May 1954. Gaer Junction, on the main line, is the Junction for the Western Valleys.

A 5600 class 0-6-2 tank, passes the comparatively new Spencer Steel Works at Llanwern, east of Newport with a down freight in 1963.

Severn Tunnel Junction, with an unidentified 'Grange' class 4-6-0 diverging from the Gloucester line with a Portsmouth train in May 1958.

A Paignton to Liverpool express passes over the troughs near Severn Tunnel Junction, in charge of one of the 'Castle' class 4-6-0's, No. 5004 *Llanstephan Castle*, June 1956.

At nearby Undy, 2800 class 2-8-0 No. 2894 heads eastwards with a freight, also in June 1956.

Two glimpses of rural South Wales at Torpantau on the former Brecon and Merthyr line in 1959. Above, 2251 class 0-6-0 No. 2280 enters with the last train of the day from Brecon to Newport. Opposite, up and down Brecon and Newport trains cross, the latter in charge of 5700 class 0-6-0 PT No. 7736.

A final memory, as a Cardiff to Pontypridd auto train disappears beneath a viaduct carrying the Cadoxton to Tonteg Junction line. The train itself is on the single line St. Fagans - Tyn-y-caeau Junction connection.